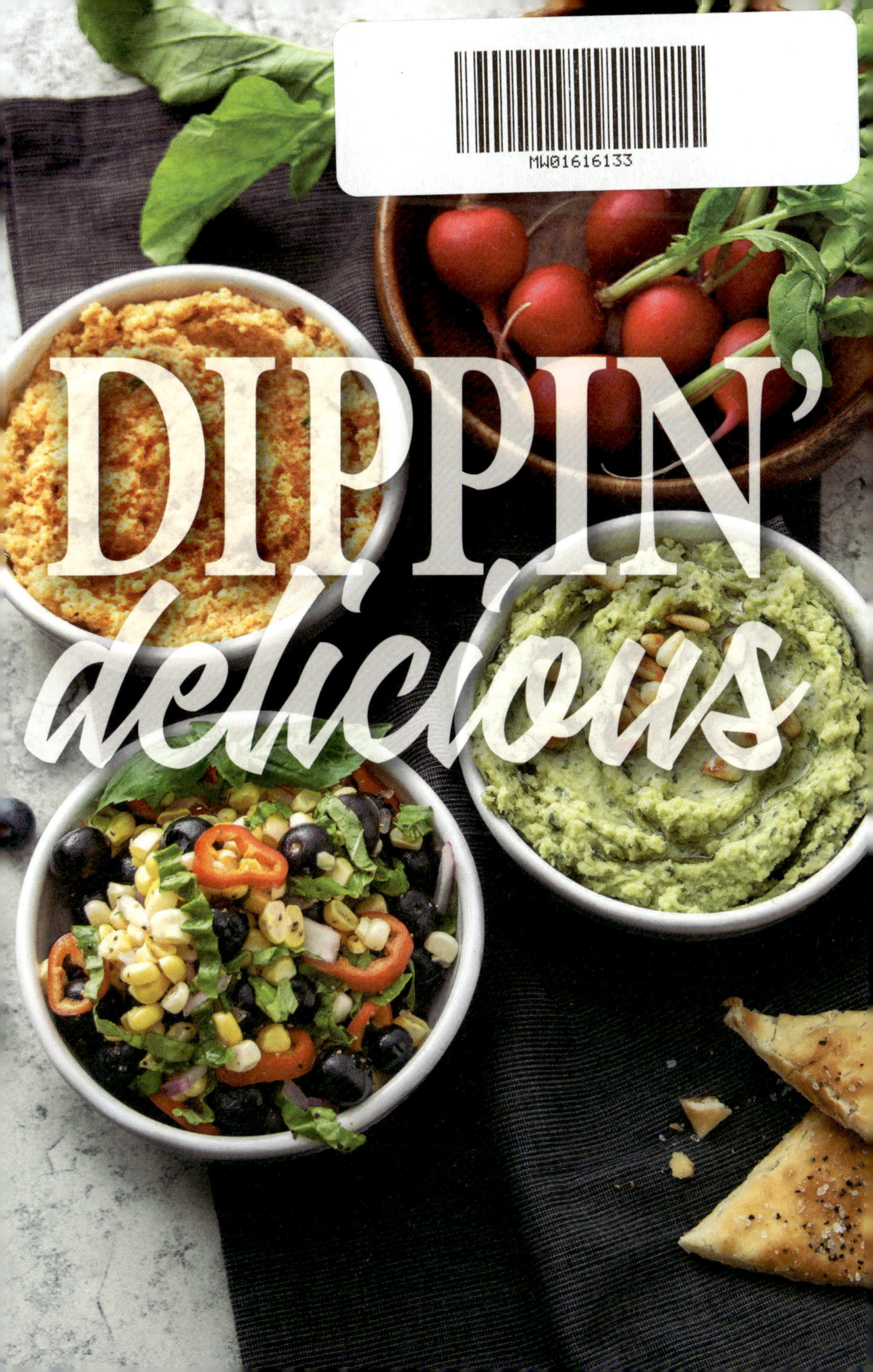

DIPPIN'
delicious

ISBN-13: 978-1-56383-649-7
Item #7158

Printed in the USA

Distributed By:

PO Box 850
Waverly, IA 50677

www.cqbookstore.com

gifts@cqbookstore.com

 CQ Products

 CQ Products

 @cqproducts

 @cqproducts

Dip Tips

Make 'Em Ahead. Most cold dips can be made hours ahead of time, then just pull them out of the fridge and serve. Plus, most cold dips taste better when they've had some time to chill, so it's basically a win-win. Hot dips can also be made ahead of time, just premix the ingredients and toss in the fridge until you're ready to heat it up.

Keep 'Em Hot. Slow cookers are an obvious choice for keeping dips hot, but not all dips are meant to be served in a slow cooker. If you're serving a baked dip, wrap towels or hot pads around the skillet or baking dish for extra insulation.

Keep 'Em Cold. It's important to keep cold dips cold – especially if you're serving mayo- or dairy-based dips on a hot day! To keep your dip chilled, just fill a larger bowl with ice and nestle your serving dish on top.

Keep 'Em Fresh. Add crunchy toppings and fresh garnishes to dips right before serving. If you're traveling, just bring your toppings along and finish the dip when you arrive. If you need to make an avocado-based dip ahead of time, press plastic wrap against the surface of the dip to eliminate air exposure. This should minimize any browning.

Go On, Get Dippin'!

Mango-Peach Salsa

1 diced mango

1 diced peach

¼ C. chopped fresh cilantro

1 jalapeño, finely diced

½ red bell pepper, diced

½ red onion, diced

1 T. lemon juice

2 T. lime juice

1 diced avocado

1 tsp. sea salt

½ tsp. black pepper

In a mixing bowl, stir together the mango, peach, cilantro, jalapeño, red bell pepper, onion, lemon juice, and lime juice. Add the avocado, salt, and black pepper and gently stir to combine. Serve with Chili-Lime Chips. **Serves 6**

Chili-Lime Chips

Preheat oven to 350°.

Stack **10 corn tortillas** and cut into 6 wedges. Lay the tortilla wedges on a baking sheet.

In a bowl, mix together **2 T. olive oil**, **2 T. lime juice**, and **2 tsp. chili powder**. Brush the oil mixture onto the tops of the corn tortilla triangles. Flip the triangles and brush the other side.

Bake for 10 to 12 minutes or until chips are firm and lightly browned. Let cool. Sprinkle with **1 T. lime juice** and **1 tsp. salt** before serving. **Makes 60 chips**

Creamy Balsamic Bruschetta

Combine **1 (8 oz.) pkg. cream cheese**, **½ tsp. garlic salt**, **1 tsp. dried parsley**, and **½ tsp. black pepper** in a small bowl; mix thoroughly. Spread evenly onto a plate or small serving platter. Refrigerate until ready to use.

In a separate bowl, combine **4 diced Roma tomatoes**, **¼ C. diced red onion**, **1 minced garlic clove**, **8 thinly sliced basil leaves**, **2 tsp. balsamic vinegar**, **1 tsp. olive oil**, **¼ tsp. salt**, and **¼ tsp. black pepper**. Cover and refrigerate for at least 30 minutes to allow the flavors to develop. When ready to serve, spread the bruschetta over the top of the cream cheese mixture. Garnish with extra basil and serve with crackers or slices of toasted baguette. **Serves 6**

Corn & Bacon Dip

6 strips bacon, chopped

3 C. frozen corn, thawed

½ C. diced onion

¼ C. diced red bell pepper

1 jalapeño, seeded & diced

4 oz. cream cheese, cubed

¼ C. sour cream

2 green onions, thinly sliced

1 tsp. sugar

¼ tsp. salt

½ tsp. black pepper

Cook bacon until brown and crispy, about 6 to 8 minutes. Transfer to a paper towel-lined plate to cool and drain the excess grease.

In a large mixing bowl, combine bacon, corn, onion, bell pepper, jalapeño, cream cheese, sour cream, green onions, sugar, salt, and black pepper. Refrigerate for at least 1 hour before serving to allow the flavors to develop. Serve with crackers or tortilla chips. **Serves 8**

Reuben Dip

1 (8 oz.) pkg. cream cheese, softened

½ C. sour cream

½ C. Thousand Island dressing

1 (14.5 oz.) can sauerkraut, drained

1 C. chopped corned beef

1 C. shredded Swiss cheese, divided

¼ C. chopped green onions, plus more for garnish

Preheat oven to 350°. In a mixing bowl, stir together the cream cheese, sour cream, and Thousand Island dressing until combined. Add the sauerkraut, corned beef, ½ cup cheese, and green onions; stir to combine. Transfer to an oven-safe baking dish and top with the remaining ½ cup cheese. Bake until bubbly and golden, about 20 minutes. Garnish with green onions before serving. Serve with toasted marble rye bread.

Slow cooker instructions: transfer the dip mixture into a slow cooker and cook on low for about 2 hours, stirring occasionally. **Serves 8**

The unbaked dip can be refrigerated overnight.

Tomato & Feta Dip

In a large mixing bowl, gently toss together **1½ C. diced Roma tomatoes**, **¼ C. finely chopped green onion**, **1 (8 oz.) pkg. crumbled feta cheese**, **¼ C. sliced Kalamata olives**, **¼ tsp. minced garlic**, **¼ tsp. black pepper**, **¼ tsp. dried dill**, and **¼ tsp. dried marjoram**. Cover and refrigerate for at least an hour before serving to allow the flavors to develop.

Before serving, spread the dip onto a small plate or dish. Finish with a light drizzle of **olive oil** and **balsamic vinegar**. Garnish with a sprig of fresh basil. Serve with crackers, flatbread, or pita chips. **Serves 6**

Molten Brie & Onion Dip

Heat **2 T. olive oil** in a skillet over medium heat. Add **1 thinly sliced yellow onion** and reduce the heat to low. Allow the onions to caramelize slowly, stirring occasionally until they are a deep golden brown. Once the onions are caramelized, deglaze the pan with **¼ C. apple cider**. Scrape up any stuck-on bits and stir into the onions.

Remove the rind from **2 (8 oz.) wheels of Brie cheese** and cut into small chunks. Turn off the heat and stir in the brie cheese until melted. Season with **salt** and **pepper** to taste. Transfer to a serving dish and sprinkle **fresh chives** on top. Serve with bread and crackers. **Serves 8**

Zippy Pepperoncini Spread

1 (8 oz.) pkg. cream cheese, softened

½ C. crumbled feta cheese

2 T. olive oil

1 T. juice from jar of pepperoncini peppers

½ tsp. black pepper

½ tsp. red pepper flakes

1 garlic clove, minced

½ C. chopped pepperoncini peppers

1 T. chopped fresh chives

Beat cream cheese, feta cheese, oil, pepperoncini juice, black pepper, red pepper flakes, and garlic with an electric mixer until smooth. Add the peppers and chives and mix until completely incorporated. Chill before serving to allow the flavors to develop. Serve with crackers.
Makes 2 cups

BLT Dip

1 (8 oz.) pkg. cream cheese, softened

¾ C. mayo

2 T. ranch seasoning

¾ C. finely shredded romaine lettuce

1 C. diced tomatoes, seeded

5 strips bacon, cooked & crumbled

¼ C. sliced green onions

Beat the cream cheese with an electric mixer until smooth. Add the mayo and ranch seasoning and beat until fully combined.

Spread the ranch mixture into the bottom of a plate or dish. Top the ranch mixture with lettuce, tomatoes, bacon and sliced green onions. Serve with crackers or toasted bread. **Serves 8**

Tiramisu Dip

Beat **1 (8 oz.) pkg. softened cream cheese** and **¾ C. mascarpone cheese** with an electric mixer on medium speed until smooth. Add **½ C. powdered sugar** and mix for 1 minute. Add **1 tsp. vanilla extract** and **2 tsp. instant coffee** and mix until fully incorporated. Scoop the dip into a serving dish and sprinkle with **cocoa powder**. Serve with vanilla wafers, fruit, or pretzels. **Makes 2 cups**

Peppered Herb Spread

Beat **1 (8 oz.) pkg. softened cream cheese** and **1 (4 oz.) pkg. goat cheese** with an electric mixer on medium speed until smooth. Add **3 T. finely chopped fresh chives**, **3 T. finely chopped fresh basil**, **3 T. finely chopped fresh parsley**, **½ tsp. cracked black pepper**, **¼ tsp. red pepper flakes**, and **1 clove minced garlic** and beat until combined. Transfer to a serving dish and refrigerate for at least 1 hour before serving to allow the flavors to develop. Serve with crackers or veggies. **Makes about 2 cups**

Goat Cheese & Tomato Dip

1 C. canned fire-roasted tomatoes

3 garlic cloves, minced

1 tsp. sugar

½ tsp. red pepper flakes

½ tsp. black pepper

¼ tsp. salt

½ tsp. paprika

4 oz. fresh goat cheese

fresh parsley for garnish

Preheat the broiler. In a small bowl, mix the fire-roasted tomatoes, garlic, sugar, red pepper flakes, black pepper, salt, and paprika. Transfer to an oven-safe dish.

Slice the fresh goat cheese and dollop over the top of the sauce. Place under the broiler and cook for about 5 minutes or until the cheese begins to bubble. Garnish with fresh parsley and serve with sliced bread. **Serves 4**

Zesty Caesar Dip

1 (8 oz.) pkg. cream cheese, softened

1 C. Caesar salad dressing, plus more for garnish

½ C. grated Parmesan cheese, divided

¼ tsp. salt

¼ tsp. black pepper

1¼ C. cubed chicken breast, cooked

2 C. chopped romaine lettuce

½ C. chopped croutons

Beat the cream cheese, salad dressing, ¼ cup Parmesan, salt, and black pepper with an electric mixer until fully incorporated. Spread the mixture in the bottom of a 9" dish.

Top the cream cheese mixture with the chicken and lettuce. Sprinkle with the remaining Parmesan and croutons, then drizzle with a little Caesar salad dressing. Serve with Baguette Garlic Toast. **Serves 8**

Baguette Garlic Toast

Preheat the oven to 375°. Slice a **baguette loaf** into ½"-thick pieces and lay in a single layer on a baking sheet. Cut a **clove of garlic** in half and rub the cut side on each piece of bread. Brush the bread with olive oil and bake for 10 minutes or until crispy. Let cool slightly. **Makes about 20 slices**

Cookie Dough Dip

1 (8 oz.) pkg. cream cheese, softened

½ C. unsalted butter, softened

1 tsp. vanilla extract

1 C. creamy peanut butter

3 T. brown sugar

1 C. powdered sugar

½ C. oatmeal

½ C. miniature M&Ms

1 C. miniature semisweet chocolate chips

With an electric mixer, beat the cream cheese, butter, vanilla, and peanut butter until smooth. Mix in the brown sugar and powdered sugar until combined. Next fold in oatmeal, M&Ms, and chocolate chips.

Serve with graham crackers, fruit, or pretzels. **Makes about 3 cups**

Supreme Italian Sub Dip

Chop **1 medium onion, 2 pickled banana peppers, ½ head iceberg lettuce, 1 big tomato** *(seeded)*, **1 (3 oz.) pkg. thinly sliced Genoa salami, 1 (7 oz.) pkg. thinly sliced deli ham, 1 (7 oz.) pkg. thinly sliced roasted turkey breast,** and **¼ lb. thinly sliced white cheddar cheese** and toss into a bowl.

In a separate bowl, whisk together **½ C. mayo, 1 T. olive oil, 1 tsp. dried oregano, 1½ tsp. dried basil,** and **¼ tsp. red pepper flakes;** add the meat to the mixture, stirring until combined. Chill until ready to serve.

Carve out the center of a round bread loaf *(we used ciabatta)*, keeping the sides and bottom intact. Pack the dip into the hollowed-out bread. Cut the ciabatta bread scraps and 8 hoagie rolls into bite-sized chunks to use for dipping. **Serves 8**

Cucumber Cream Cheese

Cube **½ cucumber** and slice **3 green onions**. Process the cucumbers and onions in a food processor until coarsely chopped. Add **1 (8 oz.) pkg. softened cream cheese, 1 tsp. Worcestershire sauce, ¼ tsp. garlic powder, ¼ tsp. salt,** and **¼ tsp. black pepper** and process until smooth. Transfer to a bowl and refrigerate for at least 1 hour to allow the flavors to develop. Serve with crackers, pretzels, or veggies. **Makes 1½ cups**

Jalapeño Popper Dip

10 strips bacon

1 (8 oz.) pkg. cream cheese, softened

⅓ C. mayo

⅓ C. sour cream

1 tsp. garlic powder

1 tsp. dried minced onion

2 jalapeños, minced, divided

1½ C. shredded cheddar cheese, divided

1½ C. shredded Monterey Jack cheese, divided

½ tsp. seasoned salt

¼ tsp. black pepper

Preheat oven to 350°. In a skillet over medium heat, cook bacon until crispy, about 8 minutes; drain and chop.

Stir together the cream cheese, mayo, sour cream, garlic powder, minced onion, bacon *(reserve some for topping)*, jalapeños *(reserve some for topping)*, and 1 cup each cheddar and Monterey Jack. Season with seasoned salt and black pepper.

Transfer to a small oven-safe skillet or baking dish and sprinkle with remaining cheese, bacon, and jalapeño. Bake until golden and bubbly, about 15 to 20 minutes. Serve with crackers. **Serves 8**

Mustard Pretzel Dip

1 C. sour cream

1 C. mayo

1 C. yellow mustard

1 T. sugar

1 T. dried minced onion

1 pkg. ranch seasoning

1 tsp. paprika

1 T. prepared horseradish

Combine all ingredients and stir until well combined. Cover and refrigerate for at least 30 minutes to allow the flavors to develop. Serve with pretzels, veggies, or crackers.
Makes 3 cups

Strawberry Bruschetta

Stir together **1½ C. sliced fresh strawberries**, **1 diced peach**, **1 C. diced cherry tomatoes**, **¼ C. thinly sliced fresh basil**, **1 diced shallot**, **1 T. olive oil**, **2 T. balsamic vinegar**, **1 tsp. black pepper**, and **¼ tsp. salt**. Crumble **1 (4 oz.) pkg. goat cheese** into small pieces and add to the bruschetta mixture; gently fold to combine. Serve with toasted baguette or crackers. **Makes about 3 cups**

Stuffed 'Shroom Dip

1 T. olive oil

½ lb. ground Italian sausage

2 garlic cloves, minced

1½ lbs. white button mushrooms, roughly chopped (about 5 C.)

Salt & freshly ground black pepper to taste

1 (8 oz.) pkg. cream cheese, cut into cubes

½ C. grated Parmesan cheese

⅓ C. half & half

½ C. chopped green onions

2 T. unsalted butter, melted

¼ C. panko bread crumbs

¼ C. fresh parsley, chopped

Preheat the broiler.

Heat the oil in a large skillet over medium-high heat. Add the sausage and cook, breaking into bite-size pieces, until browned and almost cooked through. Add the garlic and cook, stirring constantly, until softened. Add in the mushrooms, salt and a few grinds of black pepper and cook, stirring occasionally, until the mushrooms are soft and the moisture has evaporated.

Add the cream cheese and stir until melted. Add the Parmesan, half & half, and green onions and cook, stirring occasionally, until bubbly. Pour the mushroom mixture into an oven-safe dish. Mix the butter with the panko and parsley and sprinkle on top of the mushroom mixture. Broil until the bread crumbs are golden brown and the dip is bubbly around the edges, 5 to 10 minutes. Let sit for 10 minutes, then serve with crackers or bread. **Serves 8**

Flamin' Sausage Queso

Preheat oven to 350°.

Brown **½ lb. spicy pork sausage**, crumbling it while it cooks; drain and dump into a 2-qt. baking dish. Stir in **¾ C. chicken broth**, **16 oz. Velveeta** *(cubed)*, **½ C. shredded Pepper Jack cheese**, **1 (14.5 oz.) can Mexican seasoned tomatoes** *(undrained)*, and **1 C. black beans** *(drained & rinsed)*. Bake for 30 minutes, or until the cheese is melted and everything is nice and hot. Stir in **¼ C. chopped fresh cilantro**. Serve with **nacho cheese flavored tortilla chips**.

To make in a slow cooker, simply toss the browned and drained pork with the other ingredients into a 2-qt. cooker; heat on high for 2 to 3 hours. **Serves a crowd**

Mediterranean Salsa

1 (10.5 oz.) can chickpeas, drained

1 garlic clove, minced

½ C. diced cucumber

1 C. diced tomato

½ C. diced Kalamata olives

¼ C. diced red onion

1 T. chopped fresh parsley

¼ tsp. dried oregano

½ tsp. dried dill

1 T. chopped fresh basil

1 T. lemon juice

1 T. extra virgin olive oil

½ tsp. salt

½ tsp. black pepper

Add all the ingredients to a bowl and toss to combine. Serve immediately or refrigerate until ready to serve. Serve with pita chips or tortilla chips.
Serves 6

Crab Rangoon Dip

1 (8 oz.) pkg. cream cheese, softened

¼ C. mayo

¼ C. sour cream

1 C. shredded Monterey Jack cheese, divided

¼ C. shredded Parmesan cheese

3 green onions, sliced

2 tsp. Worcestershire sauce

2 tsp. soy sauce

1 tsp. Sriracha sauce

½ tsp. garlic powder

Salt & black pepper to taste

12 oz. imitation crab meat

Preheat oven to 350°. Lightly coat a 9" baking dish or cast-iron skillet with nonstick spray.

In a large bowl, combine cream cheese, mayo and sour cream. Stir in ½ cup Monterey Jack cheese, Parmesan, green onions, Worcestershire, soy sauce, Sriracha, garlic powder, and salt and pepper. Fold in the imitation crab meat.

Transfer to the prepared baking dish; top with remaining ½ cup Monterey Jack cheese. Bake until bubbly and golden, about 20 to 25 minutes. Serve with crackers or veggies. **Serves 8**

Sesame-Ginger Guac

Peel, pit, and dice **3 ripe avocados** and toss into a mixing bowl; mash with a fork. Add **1 T. rice vinegar**, **1 T. lime juice**, **1 T. soy sauce**, **1 T. sesame oil**, **2 tsp. freshly grated ginger**, **2 finely sliced green onions**, and **¼ tsp. red pepper flakes**; gently stir to combine. Garnish with sesame seeds and green onions. Serve immediately with tortilla chips, pita chips, or fresh veggies. **Makes about 2 cups**

Sizzlin' Buffalo Ranch Dip

Preheat the oven to 375°. In a large bowl, mix **1 (8 oz.) pkg. cream cheese, ½ C. buffalo-style hot sauce, ½ C. sour cream**, and **¼ C. ranch dressing** until combined. Stir in **1 C. cooked chicken, 1½ C. shredded Monterey Jack cheese**, and **¼ C. finely sliced green onions**. Scrape the mixture into a medium cast iron skillet or oven-safe dish and sprinkle **½ C. shredded montery jack cheese** on top.

Bake the dip for 20 minutes, until bubbling. Turn on the broiler and broil 6 inches from the heat until lightly browned on top. Let cool for 5 minutes before garnishing with green onions. Serve with chips, crackers, or veggies.

Tip: The unbaked dip can be refrigerated overnight. Let stand at room temperature for 20 minutes before baking. **Serves 8**

Cream Cheese & Lox

1 (8 oz.) pkg. cream cheese,
    softened

½ C. sour cream

½ tsp. garlic powder

1 tsp. dried minced onion

½ tsp. poppy seeds

½ tsp. sesame seeds,
    plus more for garnish

¼ red onion, finely chopped

3 oz. lox, chopped

1 T. capers, roughly chopped
    (optional)

1 tsp. chopped fresh dill,
    plus more for garnish

Stir together the cream cheese, sour cream, garlic powder, minced onion, poppy seeds, sesame seeds, red onion, lox, capers, and fresh dill. Refrigerate for 30 minutes to allow flavors to develop. Garnish with fresh dill and sesame seeds. Serve with bagels or bagel chips. **Makes about 2 cups**

5-Cheese Artichoke Dip

1 (16 oz.) jar roasted sweet red peppers, drained & chopped

1 (6.5 oz.) jar marinated quartered artichoke hearts, drained & chopped

1 (10 oz.) pkg. frozen chopped spinach, thawed & squeezed dry

1½ C. shredded Parmesan cheese

1 (8 oz.) pkg. cream cheese, softened & cubed

1 C. crumbled feta cheese

1 C. shredded provolone cheese, divided

⅓ C. minced fresh basil

¼ C. finely chopped red onion

2 T. mayo

2 garlic cloves, minced

½ tsp. black pepper

½ tsp. salt

8 oz. fresh mozzarella cheese, cubed

Mix the peppers, artichokes, spinach, Parmesan, cream cheese, feta, provolone, basil, onion, mayo, garlic, black pepper, and salt in a large mixing bowl. Transfer the mixture to an oven-safe baking dish and top with the cubed mozzarella. Bake until bubbly and golden, about 25 minutes. Serve with crackers or bread. **Serves a crowd**

Caramelized Onion Jam

Pour **3 T. olive oil** into the bottom of a heavy pot over medium heat. Add **3 thinly sliced white onions** and **2 tsp. minced garlic**; cook uncovered for 10 minutes, stirring every few minutes.

Add **2 T. whole grain mustard**, **¼ C. brown sugar**, **2 T. honey**, **¼ C. balsamic vinegar**, **2 C. beef broth**, **¼ tsp. dried thyme**, **¼ tsp. black pepper**, and **¼ tsp. salt**; stir to combine. Cover the pot, lower the heat slightly, and let the mixture simmer for 30 minutes.

Uncover the pot, stir, and cook until most of the liquid is gone and the onions reach a jam-like consistency, approximately 50 minutes. Serve hot or cold with crackers or bread. **Makes about 1 cup**

Cranberry-Pistachio Cheese Ball

1 (8 oz.) pkg. cream cheese, softened

2 C. shredded Monterey Jack cheese

1 tsp. Dijon mustard

1 tsp. Worcestershire sauce

1 T. dried parsley

½ tsp. salt

½ tsp. black pepper

½ C. dried cranberries, roughly chopped

½ C. roughly chopped pistachios

Beat the cream cheese, Monterey Jack, Dijon, Worcestershire, parsley, salt, and black pepper with an electric mixer until combined. Mix in the cranberries. Cover and refrigerate until slightly firm, 1 to 2 hours.

Transfer the cheese mixture to a piece of plastic wrap. Use the plastic to shape the cheese mixture into a ball. Remove the plastic and cover the cheeseball with pistachios, pressing to adhere. Wrap in plastic wrap and chill until ready to serve. Serve with crackers. **Serves 8**

Green Goddess Dip

2 C. packed arugula

½ C. fresh basil leaves

3 T. chopped fresh chives

1 T. chopped fresh parsley

½ tsp. lemon zest

½ C. mayo

¼ C. sour cream

1 tsp. Dijon mustard

2 garlic cloves

¼ tsp. salt

¼ tsp. black pepper

Combine the arugula, basil, chives, parsley, and lemon zest in a food processor; process for 10 seconds. Add the mayo, sour cream, Dijon mustard, garlic, salt, and black pepper. Process until all ingredients are finely chopped. Cover and chill for at least an hour before serving to allow the flavors to develop. Serve with veggies and crackers.
Makes 1½ cups

PB & Chocolate Hummus

In a food processor, combine **1 (16 oz.) can chickpeas** *(drained & rinsed)*, **¼ C. peanut butter**, **¼ C. honey**, **2 T. maple syrup**, **½ C. unsweetened cocoa powder**, **1 tsp. vanilla**, and **¼ tsp. salt**. Process for 30 seconds, then scrape down the sides of the bowl. Add **2 to 3 T. water** and process again until it becomes nice and creamy; chill.

Set out to soften 30 minutes before serving. Drizzle with **honey** and top with **chopped peanuts**. Serve with pretzels and fresh fruit. **Serves 6**

Double Dill Dip

Mix **1 (8 oz.) pkg. softened cream cheese** and **¼ C. pickle juice** with an electric mixer until combined. Add **1½ C. chopped dill pickles, 1 C. shredded cheddar cheese, ¼ tsp. garlic powder, ½ tsp. dried dill, ½ C. chopped Genoa salami, ¼ tsp. black pepper,** and **¼ C. diced red onion**; stir to combine. Cover and refrigerate for at least 2 hours before serving to allow the flavors to develop. Serve with crackers, pretzels, or veggies.
Makes about 4 cups

Coastal Shrimp Dip

2 T. butter

1 lb. shrimp, peeled, deveined, & coarsely chopped

1 garlic clove, minced

4 green onions, sliced

1 T. lemon juice

1 C. mayo

¼ C. sour cream

½ C. cream cheese, softened

¼ C. shredded Parmesan cheese

¼ C. minced bell pepper

2 T. finely chopped fresh parsley

½ tsp. Old Bay seasoning

¼ tsp. celery salt

¼ tsp. black pepper

1 C. mozzarella cheese

Preheat the oven to 350°. Melt butter in a skillet over medium heat. Add shrimp, garlic, and onions and cook just until the shrimp are pink. Stir in lemon juice and remove from heat.

Combine the shrimp mixture, mayo, sour cream, cream cheese, Parmesan, bell pepper, parsley, Old Bay, celery salt, and black pepper. Transfer to an oven-safe dish and top with mozzarella. Bake until golden and bubbly, about 20 to 25 minutes. Serve with bread or crackers. **Serves 8**

Pesto Hummus

2 (14 oz.) cans chickpeas, drained & rinsed

½ C. fresh basil leaves, plus more for garnish

¼ C. grated Parmesan cheese

¼ C. olive oil, plus more for garnish

1 T. pine nuts, plus more for garnish

3 garlic cloves, minced

Juice of 1 lemon

½ tsp. black pepper

Salt to taste

Combine all the ingredients except salt in a food processor and blend on high until smooth. Season with salt. Transfer the hummus to a serving dish and refrigerate for at least 30 minutes to allow flavors to develop. Garnish with basil, pine nuts, and a drizzle of olive oil before serving. Serve with Black Pepper Pita Chips.

Keep covered in your fridge for up to 5 days. **Serves 8**

Black Pepper Pita Chips

Brush **olive oil** over one side of **5 pita bread rounds**; sprinkle with **sea salt** and **coarse black pepper**. Cut each round into eight triangles and bake at 375° for 10 minutes or until toasted. **Makes 40**

Outrageous Olive Dip

1 (8 oz.) pkg. cream cheese, softened

½ C. mayo

1½ C. shredded cheddar cheese

1 garlic clove, minced

½ C. coarsely chopped pimento stuffed green olives

¼ C. chopped fresh parsley

Mix the cream cheese and mayo with an electric mixer until well combined. Add the cheese, garlic, olives, and parsley. Stir to combine. Cover and refrigerate for at least 2 hours before serving. Serve with chips, veggies, or crackers. **Makes about 2½ cups**

Refrigerator Pepper Jelly

Combine **1 finely chopped red bell pepper**, 1 finely chopped yellow bell pepper, 1 finely chopped orange bell pepper, 2 finely chopped and seeded jalapeños, 1 (1.75 oz.) pkg. fruit pectin, and ¾ C. distilled white vinegar in a saucepan over medium heat. Bring the mixture to a boil for 5 minutes, stirring frequently.

Add **4 C. sugar** and bring the mixture back to a boil; let boil for 2 minutes. Remove the pan from the heat and pour the jelly into containers. Allow to cool, uncovered, for 30 minutes. Seal and place in the refrigerator to allow the jelly to set. Refrigerate in an airtight container for up to 1 month. Serve with crackers, or pair with cream cheese for a classic appetizer. **Makes 5 cups**

Spicy Cranberry Spread

Dump **1 (12 oz.) pkg. cranberries** and **1 C. sugar** into a food processor and process briefly until coarsely chopped. Transfer the mixture to a bowl and stir in **6 chopped green onions**, **⅓ C. chopped fresh cilantro**, and **1 seeded and finely chopped jalapeño**. Cover and refrigerate overnight.

After chilling, drain the cranberry mixture. Spread **1 (8 oz.) pkg. cream cheese** on a plate and spoon the drained mixture over the top. Serve with crackers. **Serves 6**

Garlic & Herb Dip

1 C. mayo

½ C. sour cream

1 T. dried parsley

1 T. dried chives

½ tsp. dried tarragon

1 tsp. dried dill

1 tsp. minced garlic

½ tsp. dried minced onion

¼ tsp. paprika

¼ tsp. salt

¼ tsp. black pepper

Combine all ingredients in a mixing bowl. Refrigerate for several hours to allow the flavors to develop. Serve with veggies or crackers.
Makes 1½ cups

Hot Pimento Cheese Dip

8 oz. shredded sharp
   cheddar cheese

8 oz. shredded
   Monterey Jack cheese

4 oz. pimentos

1 jalapeño, diced

¼ C. diced green onions

1 tsp. ground cumin

½ C. mayo

½ C. softened cream cheese

Preheat oven to 350°.

Mix cheddar, Monterey Jack, pimentos, jalapeño, green onions, and cumin. Stir in the mayo and cream cheese until well combined. Spread the mixture evenly into a small skillet.

Bake for 20 minutes or until hot and bubbly. Serve with toasted bread, crackers, and veggies. **Serves 8**

Caramel Apple Dip

Put **½ C. chopped pecans** in a dry skillet and toast over medium heat for 8 minutes, stirring occasionally.

Set **1 (8 oz.) pkg. softened cream cheese** on a serving tray. Core and slice **4 apples** *(mix & match your favorites)* and put into a bowl; drizzle with **lemon juice**, stir to coat, and then drain. Heat **½ C. caramel sauce** in the microwave and drizzle it over the cream cheese. Top with the toasted pecans and surround with the sliced apples.

Tip: If you're in a hurry, just pour on the caramel sauce without heating and toss on the pecans without toasting. It'll still be delicious! **Serves 8**

Fresh Watermelon Salsa

In a small saucepan, whisk together **¼ C. balsamic vinegar** and **1 T. sugar**. Cook over medium heat until reduced by half and syrupy, about 4 minutes. Allow to cool.

Meanwhile stir together **3 C. diced watermelon**, **1 C. diced cucumber**, **¼ C. diced red onion**, **½ tsp. salt**, **½ tsp. black pepper**, and **¼ C. chopped fresh cilantro**. Add the balsamic reduction and **½ C. crumbled feta cheese** to the bowl and gently stir to combine. Serve with tortilla chips. **Makes about 4 cups**

Spicy Smoked Gouda Spread

2 C. finely shredded smoked
  Gouda cheese

4 oz. cream cheese, softened

¼ C. mayo

1 jalapeño, finely diced

½ tsp. paprika

½ tsp. chipotle powder

¼ tsp. salt

¼ tsp. black pepper

Stir together all ingredients until thoroughly combined. Refrigerate for at least an hour before serving to allow the flavors to develop. Serve with crackers, veggies, or bread.
Serves 6

Ultimate Street Corn Dip

2 (8 oz.) pkgs. cream cheese, softened

½ C. sour cream

2 garlic cloves, minced

2 T. hot sauce, plus more for garnish

½ tsp. paprika

Juice of 1 lime

2 C. shredded Pepper Jack cheese, divided

2 (15 oz.) cans corn, drained & rinsed

½ C. crumbled Cotija cheese, plus more for garnish

1 jalapeño, seeds removed & diced

2 T. chopped red onion

½ C. chopped fresh cilantro, plus more for garnish

Preheat oven to 350°.

Combine cream cheese, sour cream, garlic, hot sauce, paprika, lime juice, and 1 cup of the shredded cheese with an electric mixer. Blend until fully combined.

Scoop the cream cheese mixture into a large bowl and add the remaining 1 cup Pepper Jack, corn, Cotija, jalapeño, onion, and cilantro. Stir to combine.

Pour mixture into a greased baking dish.

Bake for 15 to 20 minutes or until cheese is hot and bubbly. Garnish with more cilantro, Cotija, and hot sauce.

Serve with chips and enjoy! **Serves 8**

Loaded Baked Potato Dip

8 strips bacon, cooked & crumbled

2 C. sour cream

¼ C. finely chopped green onions

1 C. shredded sharp cheddar cheese

2 garlic cloves, minced

1 tsp. dried minced onion

¼ tsp. seasoned salt

1 tsp. black pepper

Combine all ingredients in a large mixing bowl. Chill for at least one hour before serving to allow the flavors to develop. Transfer to a serving bowl and serve with potato chips. **Serves a crowd**

This will become your go-to potato chip dip!

Pineapple Cheese Ball

In a large mixing bowl, combine **2 (8 oz.) pkgs. softened cream cheese**, **1 (8 oz.) can crushed pineapple** *(drained)*, **1½ T. seasoned salt**, **1 C. chopped pecans**, **½ C. chopped bell pepper**, and **1 T. dried parsley.**

Chill the mixture until firm, 1 to 2 hours. Form the chilled mixture into 2 cheeseballs and roll in 1 C. chopped pecans, pressing to adhere. Wrap in plastic wrap until ready to serve. Serve with crackers. **Makes 2 cheeseballs**

Holy Guacamole

Peel, pit, and dice **3 ripe avocados** and toss into a bowl with
1 T. lime juice; mash with a fork to reach the desired consistency
(chunky or creamy – your call). Stir in **½ tsp. salt**, **½ tsp. ground
cumin**, **¼ tsp. cayenne pepper**, **1 T. chopped fresh cilantro**,
2 T. finely chopped red onion, **2 Roma tomatoes** *(seeded & diced)*,
½ jalapeño pepper *(seeded & finely chopped)*, and **½ tsp. minced
garlic**. Transfer to a serving bowl and sprinkle with a little black
pepper. Serve with tortilla chips or veggies. **Makes about 2 cups**

Peachy Bacon Dip

1 T. butter

½ C. thinly sliced Vidalia onion

2 strips bacon, chopped

1 tsp. black pepper

¼ tsp. salt

1 C. cola

¼ C. packed brown sugar

2 C. coarsely chopped fresh peaches,
   (about 3 to 4 peaches)

½ C. chopped pecans

2 (8 oz.) pkgs. cream cheese, softened

Melt the butter in large skillet on medium-high heat. Add onion and bacon; cook and stir 6 to 8 minutes or until bacon is crisp.

Stir black pepper, salt, cola, and brown sugar into skillet. Bring to a boil and immediately reduce heat to low; simmer 15 minutes or until mixture thickens slightly, stirring occasionally. Stir in peaches and pecans; simmer until heated through.

Spread cream cheese on the bottom of a pie plate or dish. Top with the warm peach mixture. Serve with assorted crackers or sliced bread.
Serves 10

Blueberry-Basil Salsa

2 ears raw corn, cut off the cob

1 C. blueberries

½ red onion, finely diced

3 mini sweet peppers, cut into rings

½ C. thinly sliced fresh basil

¼ tsp. black pepper

1 T. olive oil

Juice of 1 lime

Salt to taste

Toss together the raw corn, blueberries, onion, peppers, fresh basil, and black pepper. Drizzle with the olive oil and lime juice and gently stir to combine. Season to taste with salt and serve at room temperature or chilled. Serve with tortilla chips. **Makes about 2 cups**

Honey Almond Brie

Preheat oven to 350°. Use a knife to trim the thin white rind off the top of an **8 oz. wheel of Brie cheese**. Place the Brie in an oven-safe ramekin or skillet. Bake for 11 to 13 minutes or until softened. While the brie bakes, combine **¼ C. honey** and a **sprig of rosemary** in a small saucepan over low heat. Once warmed, stir in **½ C. chopped roasted almonds**. Spoon the honey mixture over the Brie and garnish with a sprig of rosemary. Serve with toasted bread.

Tip: The cheese loses its "gooeyness" relatively fast, so try to time it to come out of the oven right before serving time. **Serves 6**

Zesty Lime Dip

Beat **1 (8 oz.) pkg. softened cream cheese** in a big mixing bowl on medium speed until very creamy. Beat in **1 (14 oz.) can sweetened condensed milk**, **1 (6 oz.) container key lime yogurt**, **1 (6 oz.) container piña colada yogurt**, **1 tsp. vanilla**, and **1 T. lemon juice** until light and smooth; stir in the **zest and juice of 1 lime**. Cover and refrigerate overnight. Serve with fruit *(we used strawberries, orange segments, and pineapple chunks)*.

Tip: This recipe makes a lot of dip. Consider dividing into smaller portions and freezing some for later. Then just thaw and dip.
Makes 4 cups

Chimichurri Dip

2 garlic cloves, minced

1½ C. chopped fresh parsley

2 T. chopped fresh cilantro

5 large fresh basil leaves, chopped

½ C. olive oil

1 T. lime juice

½ tsp. red pepper flakes

Salt to taste

Black pepper to taste

Stir garlic and herbs together in a small bowl. Add the olive oil, lime juice, and red pepper flakes; stir well. Season with salt and black pepper. Serve with bread for dipping.

Tip: This dip is also delicious drizzled on top of grilled steak or chicken.
Serves 6

Orange & Avocado Salsa

1 orange, peeled & diced

1 jalapeño, seeded & finely chopped

1 C. chopped fresh cilantro

2 T. orange juice

½ tsp. salt

2 avocados, peeled & diced

In a mixing bowl, combine the orange, jalapeño, cilantro, orange juice, and salt. Add the avocado and gently stir to combine. Serve immediately with tortilla chips.
Makes about 3 cups

Cumin Hummus

In the bowl of a food processor, combine **¼ C. tahini** and **¼ C. lemon juice** and process for 1½ minutes, scraping the sides and bottom of the bowl once. Add **2 T. olive oil**, **1 minced garlic clove**, **½ tsp. ground cumin**, and **½ tsp. salt** and process for 1 minute, until well blended, scraping the bowl once. Add **1 (14 oz.) can chickpeas** *(drained & rinsed)* and process for 1 minute; scrape the bowl and continue processing until thick and quite smooth. With the food processor running, slowly add **2 T. water** through the chute, until the hummus is very smooth. Taste and add extra salt if needed. Transfer to a serving bowl, drizzle with a **little oil**, sprinkle with **paprika**, and serve with **veggies**. **Makes 2 cups**

Fruit Salsa

2 T. sugar

1 T. brown sugar

3 T. fruit preserves,
  any flavor (we used
  raspberry)

2 kiwis, peeled & diced

2 Golden Delicious apples,
  diced

1 (6 oz.) pkg. fresh
  raspberries

1 lb. fresh strawberries,
  diced

1 C. fresh blueberries

In a big bowl, mix the sugar, brown sugar, and preserves until well combined. Add the kiwis, apples, raspberries, strawberries, and blueberries; gently stir to mix. Cover and chill until ready to serve. Serve with Cinnamon Chips.
Serves a crowd

Cinnamon Chips

Preheat the oven to 350°. Coat **10 (10") tortillas** with cooking spray. Sprinkle with **cinnamon-sugar** and spritz again with cooking spray. Cut each tortilla into eight wedges and arrange in a single layer on baking sheets. Bake on the bottom oven rack for 10 to 15 minutes, until lightly browned; cool before serving. **Makes 80 chips.**

Index